199ℓ

ILLUMINAT

Visions for Change, Growth and Self-Acceptance

ILLUMINATIONS

Visions for Change, Growth and Self-Acceptance

STEPHEN C. PAUL, Ph.D.

with paintings by

GARY MAX COLLINS

HarperSanFrancisco

A Division of HarperCollins*Publishers*

ILLUMINATIONS: *Visions for Change, Growth and Self-Acceptance.*
Copyright © 1991 by Stephen C. Paul with paintings by Gary Collins. Printed in the United States of America. No part of this book may be used or reproduced in any manner whatsoever without written permission except in the case of brief quotations embodied in critical articles and reviews. For information address HarperCollins Publishers, 10 East 53rd Street, New York, NY 10022.

Design and Composition by Wilsted & Taylor

LIBRARY OF CONGRESS CATALOGING-IN-PUBLICATION DATA

Paul, Stephen C.
    Illuminations : visions for change, growth and self-acceptance /
by Stephen C. Paul with paintings by Gary Collins.
        p.   cm.
    ISBN 0-06-250681-1
    1. Self-actualization (Psychology)   2. Self-acceptance.
3. Change (Psychology)   I. Collins, Gary, 1936–   .   II. Title.
BF637.S4P3778   1990
158–dc20
                                                        90–4423
                                                        CIP

96   HCP–HK   10

This book is dedicated

to those people everywhere

who are changing . . .

and changing the world

through their changes.

This book is for those of you who, despite your fears and doubts, are always motivated forward. It's for those of you who, realizing the difficult obstacles in your life, have been making the difficult changes necessary to become who you are and to have what you want. I feel a deep respect for your commitment and admire your courage. This book is offered to you as an acknowledgment of what you are doing and as a reminder when one is needed.

The statements in the book progress from recognitions of how you masked your pain, through realizations that help you remove the mask, toward illuminations of the possibilities beyond. They reflect the process of shedding your accumulated distortions. Each statement is meant to be a challenge. Some of them will be challenges you have already met. Others may be facing you now. Some may lie in your future. They are all dedicated to supporting your pursuit of a fully conscious life, a goal I think we share.

The sayings have come to me over the years in my work with clients at many points of change. My clients were my teachers. I have always felt it was a privilege that they would share their thoughts, feelings and experiences with me. Many times, the things I found myself saying to them became my lessons. Now I pass on those lessons to you.

Gary's original paintings are meditations that amplify and elaborate the individual statements. The entire sequence of paintings follows the same expanding course set out by the sayings. They not only supplement the words in the book, but add an element of their own and represent the promise of beauty and creation that can come to illuminate your life.

My collaboration with Gary began during a late-night conversation about the many changes taking place in our own lives. Every now and then, Gary stopped me to write down one of my comments. He asked me if I would be willing to couple my thoughts with his artwork and create this book. The book has been the most enjoyable and effortless activity of my life.

ILLUMINATIONS

Visions for Change, Growth and Self-Acceptance

You too

withhold

the very things

you complain are missing

from the world.

The space for what

you want

is already filled

with what you

settle for

instead.

You live for others

and wonder why

you're never fulfilled.

When you give up

your own truth

to win

at someone else's game,

everyone loses.

Your relationships

reflect your fears

and limits.

How can anyone

ever give you

what you won't allow?

Every time you settle

for the unacceptable

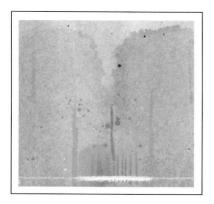

you suffer a small death.

Everything and everyone

in your life

is there

by your choice.

No one

really benefits

from your pretending.

An unrevealed part

of yourself

is never understood.

Everything

you're looking for

lies behind

the mask you wear.

Release your

snapshot images

of relationships.

Life is a motion picture.

How can anyone

ever love you

for who you are

if you become someone else

to be with them?

You can only

see others

as clearly as

you see

yourself.

Your fears

stand between you

and what you want.

They're worth

facing!

No one

has power over you

unless

you give it to them.

Is it

more important

to avoid your fear

than to be

who you are

and have

what you want?

People

will never understand you

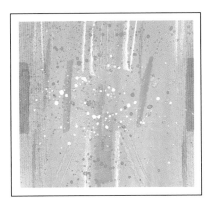

until you're willing

to let them see

who you are.

The distractions

you created

to cope

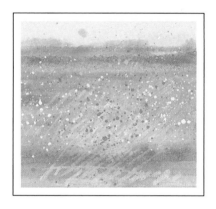

clutter your

consciousness.

If you could choose

the perfect life,

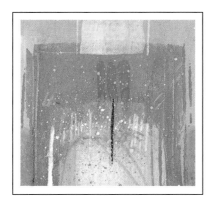

would you choose

the life you have?

You hang on to the past

hoping for what should have been

but still isn't

and never will be

until you let go!

You've suffered enough.

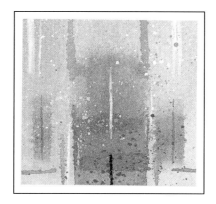

Are you ready

to try something else?

Inside

your armor

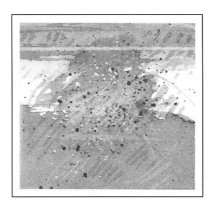

you're already

soft

and beautiful.

All you really want

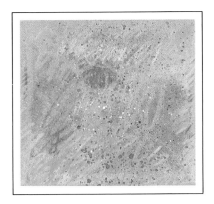

is to be loved

and accepted

for who you are.

It's easier to pretend

that you don't know what to do

than to do what you need to do.

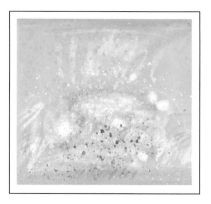

You know what to do.

Facing your fear

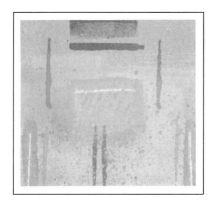

is the price

of growth.

The world reflects

what you need to see,

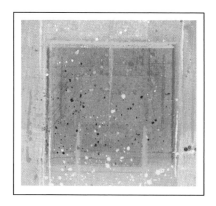

not only

what you

want to see.

You create

your life

with each choice

you make.

Recognize

that you

have done

the best you could

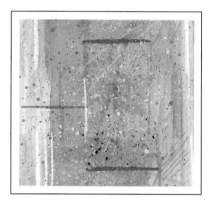

and forgive yourself.

Recognize

that everyone

has done

the best they could

and forgive them.

Trust is

your gift to give,

not something

to be earned.

You gave away

your self-esteem

in bits and pieces.

You have the power

to reclaim it.

Your beliefs

are your reality.

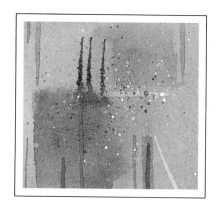

If you don't like

the reality you see,

change your beliefs!

Commitment to a relationship

requires

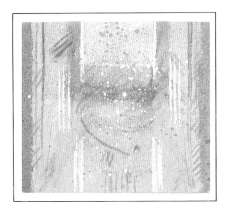

facing the issues.

Emotions pass like clouds

across the sky.

They're to be noticed,

accepted, acknowledged,

and allowed

to flow on.

You never

need to defend

or justify

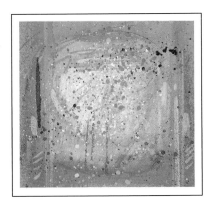

your

feelings.

The trick

is to respect yourself

and the other person

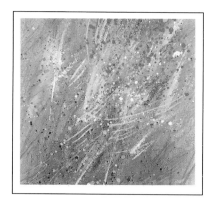

at the

same

time.

Trust because

you are willing

to accept the risk,

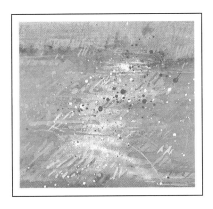

not because

it's safe

or certain.

Honor your feelings.

They tell the truth

about

how you really

experience

the world.

Nothing that you do

other than

doing what you need to do

gets it done!

The way you cope,

no matter how well

it seems to work,

is simply a mask

for the pain.

Your beliefs

select the reality

you see.

You always

have a choice,

even when it seems

you don't.

You don't get

to control

any outcome,

only every choice you make

along the way.

It's not enough

to know your truth,

you must live it!

Acknowledge

yourself

for keeping

possibility

alive.

Every time

you let go

of something limiting,

you create

space

for something better.

Surround yourself

with people

who want you to be

everything

you can be.

Once the truth

is told,

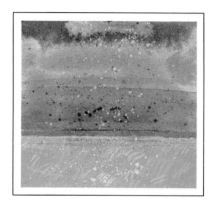

you never need

to pretend

again.

If you believed

that you deserve

everything that you want,

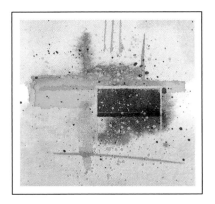

you'd have it.

You gave up getting

what you wanted

from people

who couldn't give it.

Now it's time

to risk again!

In a

good relationship,

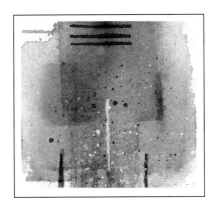

each person gives

what they want

to get.

Every time

you heal

a dark part

of yourself

you bring more light

into

the world.

To be free

yourself,

you have to release

everyone else.

Being attached

to the future

is still

attachment.

There is only pain

in resisting.

Relax and yield.

Why fight

for freedom?

You're already free.

The most important product

of your life

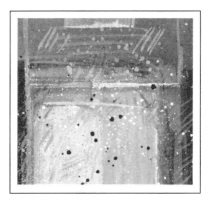

is you.

Once you accept

yourself

there's no reason

to hold

anything

back.

Make room for

yourself

in your life

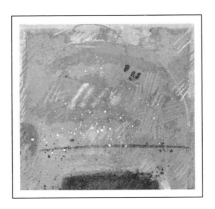

by keeping it

simple.

Always ask yourself

how everyone and everything

in your life

serves you.

Happiness

isn't

getting what you want,

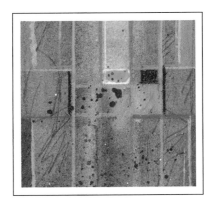

but

experiencing

who you are.

Bring yourself

uniquely and fully

into bloom . . .

Don't just

weed your garden.

After waiting

all these years,

it's time to

hope and dream

again!

Open to

the possibility

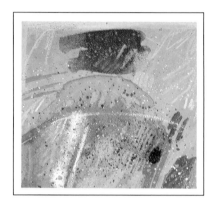

of having

everything

you want.

Discover

the difference

between

doing and being

and

become!

There is never

a frozen moment.

Life flows

and so must we.

Move

through the world

with

gentle strength.

There's incredible beauty

in the world.

Open yourself

to see it.

For all these years

you've protected

the seed.

It's time

to become

the flower.

Go often

to those places

where you

remember.

It is as important

to release

the future

as it is

to release

the past.

Compassion

for others

comes naturally

as you recognize

your own

limitations.

Be understanding

and compassionate,

but not

responsible

for others.

With each limit

you remove,

you move toward

boundless freedom.

This is

your world!

Honor it

as your own

and graciously

enjoy its gifts.

What it means

to have it all

expands

as you

expand.

Peace on earth

will come

from making peace

inside yourself

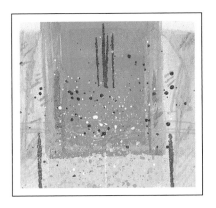

and bringing it

with you

into the world.

Let go!

Creation

takes place

in the void!

Accept

prosperity

in

every form

the universe

offers.

Discover

the unknown

in every

experience.

Rediscover

life

with the wonder

of a

child.

When you have

fulfilled yourself,

you can give

out of

abundance.

Greet everyone

and everything

as they exist

without judgment.

There are people

who will

joyfully greet

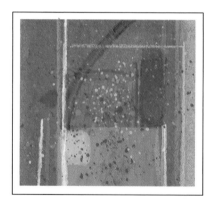

the person

you are

becoming.

Fill your life

with good company.

One day

you realize

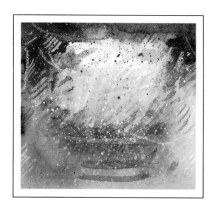

you have

nothing

to prove.

It's important

to remain

lighthearted.

The earth

becomes heaven

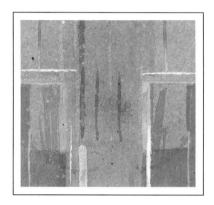

when you release

your fear.

What a joy

to recognize

yourself

in someone else's

eyes.

It's impossible

to have too much

fun.

The greatest gift

you give

to the universe

is being

who

you really are.

Creation,

after all,

is only

play.

You can tell

that you're doing

the right thing

if it feels

effortless.

Allow

the earth

to be

a part of heaven.

Your expression

in all its forms

is the dance

of creation.

Don't forget

to fly!